W9-CDO-975

DISCARDED
from
New Hanover County Public Library

NORTH CAROLINA'S SIGNERS

Brief Sketches of the Men Who Signed the Declaration of Independence and the Constitution

By
Memory F. Mitchell

DISCARDED New Hanover County Public Library

NEW HANOVER COUNTY PUBLIC LIBRARY

RALEIGH
DIVISION OF ARCHIVES AND HISTORY
NORTH CAROLINA DEPARTMENT OF CULTURAL RESOURCES
1964
Third Printing, 1980

ISBN 0-86526-097-4

DEPARTMENT OF CULTURAL RESOURCES
Sara W. Hodgkins
Secretary

DIVISION OF ARCHIVES AND HISTORY
Larry E. Tise
Director

NORTH CAROLINA HISTORICAL COMMISSION
Sarah M. Lemmon, *Chairman*

Dick Brown
Gertrude S. Carraway
T. Harry Gatton
Raymond Gavins
Samuel W. Johnson

Harley E. Jolley
H. G. Jones
R. M. Lineberger
Clyde M. Norton
John E. Raper, Jr.

PREFACE

For many years the Division of Archives and History, North Carolina Department of Cultural Resources, and its predecessor agencies have published pamphlets on North Carolina history. The staff of the Historical Publications Section, which is responsible for the production of the pamphlets, would like to update, modernize, and enlarge some of the earlier publications; but limited staff and funds for printing prevent extensive revision. Rather than let titles go out of print, many of the older pamphlets have been reprinted several times with only minor changes.

In this edition of *North Carolina's Signers*, a few errors have been corrected and the twenty-sixth amendment to the United States Constitution has been added on page 54.

Former members of the staff of the Historical Publications Section, Mrs. Betsy J. Gunter, Mrs. Catherine G. Barnhardt, Mrs. Brenda C. Whicker, and the late Elizabeth W. Wilborn and Doris Critcher assisted in preparation of copy for the press. Unless otherwise indicated, photographs used herein are from the files of the Division of Archives and History.

Memory F. Mitchell
Historical Publications Administrator

July 1, 1980

CONTENTS

Illustrations

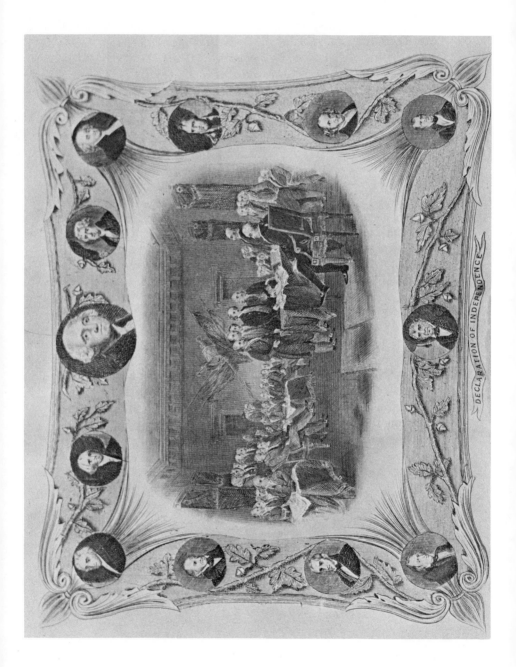

DECLARATION OF INDEPENDENCE

Background for Independence and Contribution of Delegates

North Carolinians have every reason to be proud of the role played by their early leaders in the struggle for independence from Great Britain. The men who represented the State at the Continental Congress and at the Federal Convention were experienced and intelligent. They were mature, although their average age was less than forty years: William Richardson Davie at thirty was the youngest and Hugh Williamson at fifty-one was the oldest. They were individuals although they shared a common task. William Blount and Alexander Martin seldom voiced their opinions; Davie and Richard Dobbs Spaight spoke more often; Williamson was the most voluble delegate, making 73 speeches, offering 23 motions, seconding the motions of others, and serving on many committees.

Fifty-six men signed the Declaration of Independence—among them Joseph Hewes, William Hooper, and John Penn; thirty-nine signatures are on the Constitution of the United States—including those of Blount, Spaight, and Williamson of North Carolina. These are names to be revered long after the documents have crumpled to dust and the ink has vanished.

The concept of freedom as it was envisioned by the founding fathers has since served to unshackle bonds in many parts of the world. Such a concept was unknown in 1776, when kings felt that they were due only obedience from their colonies. What finally caused the people to reach the decision to sever the ties of the Mother Country?

Independence from Great Britain was not an impulsive action resulting from mass hysteria. It had been talked at firesides, in the churches, on the lonely trails, along the wharfs and piers, in the fields, at formal balls, and at cabin play-parties. Freedom was often the subject of lengthy debate in legislative halls, and there were many who confessed that they often lay sleepless, planning and thinking of the risks involved. By April 12, 1776, the time of talking had passed; action was the only decision possible. North Carolinians dared to act while others hesitated!

The men and women who came to settle the New World had left their homeland for many reasons: to escape injustice, to find intellectual freedom, to take advantage of the opportunities offered them and their children, and in many instances to rise above their station in life, possible only in a new land. North Carolina was settled by people who had one or more of these reasons. Many of the citizens had

Signers of the Declaration of Independence. From *The Century of Independence ... Documents and Statistics Connected with the Political History of America*, frontispiece.

left an easier life in neighboring colonies. Just as the geography of the colony differed from that of others, so did the character of the people.

Several of the colonies had an almost entirely English citizenry; North Carolina had more English than any other nationality, but it also had more non-English white people than any other southern colony. Its population was less concentrated in coastal towns; its settlers had pushed farther into the back-country. In a colony larger than that of New York, there were Swiss, German, Scotch-Irish, French Huguenot, and Negro, as well as the hardy English yeomen. Spread throughout the Coastal Plain and Piedmont these stubborn pioneers were, under the leadership of Henderson and Boone, opening the mountain gaps. There were more small industries, more small farms and farmers, and there was more chafing against English rule than in South Carolina and Virginia.

Here dwelt a people who refused to accept the dictates of king and parliament: They refused to co-operate with their governors—proprietary and royal—taking a perverse delight in procrastinating in complying with or totally obstructing the laws passed by the General Assembly. In fairness it should be noted that these governors were for the most part honest men, who were poorly paid for their services. For at least 40 years before the Revolution North Carolinians had shown their displeasure with authority. They were anxious to get rid of the Stamp Act, the Navigation Acts, the Sugar Act, the "Intolerable Acts," and any other restrictive measures. These people had claimed an unfriendly territory; they had fought the wily Indian; they had established trade and opened poor harbors using the rich stores available from nature; they had refused to accept the Church of England and kept their own religious beliefs—they would act now! They would not stand by any longer and permit further infringement of their personal liberties.

Halifax Resolves

The effects of these political and economic developments were felt strongly in North Carolina. Full accounts of the events leading to the Revolution may be read in other books,* but by April, 1776, sentiment in favor of independence was prevalent here. North Carolina's Fourth Provincial Congress, held in Halifax beginning on April 4, was attended by delegates who realized that a break with Great Britian was imminent. A committee was appointed to consider the various grievances and to draw appropriate resolutions. This report was

---

* For North Carolina's role, see Hugh F. Rankin, *North Carolina in the American Revolution* (Raleigh: State Department of Archives and History, 1959).

unanimously adopted on April 12, and the document is now known as the Halifax Resolves.

The Provincial Congress of North Carolina instructed its delegates in Philadelphia "to concur with the delegates of other Colonies in declaring Independency, and forming foreign alliances, reserving to this colony the sole and exclusive right of forming a Constitution and laws for this Colony. . . ."

A copy of the Halifax Resolves was sent to Joseph Hewes, one of North Carolina's representatives in the Congress. Newspapers throughout the colonies printed the text of the document and praised the action taken by the North Carolina group. On May 15 Virginia instructed her delegates to work for independence, and on May 27 the delegates from Virginia and those from North Carolina presented their instruction to the Congress. A motion was made on June 7 that the United States should be free and independent; Congress adopted the resolution on July 2, and two days later approved the final draft of the document, called the Declaration of Independence

North Carolina's Delegates to Philadelphia

Joseph Hewes, John Penn, and William Hooper were North Carolina's delegates to the Second Continental Congress at Philadelphia. They played significant roles in the actions of the Congress, and representing North Carolina they signed their names to the historic document that resulted from their meeting. A brief study of the lives of these three men and others like them is an opportunity to learn about North Carolina's leaders in the formative years of her history.

Joseph Hewes

Joseph Hewes' parents were Quakers. They were married in Connecticut in 1728 but the Indian massacres and the lack of religious toleration shortly forced them to move to New Jersey. Mrs. Hewes was wounded in an Indian attack as they traveled. They settled on a small farm and there Joseph was born on January 23, 1730. Hewes was a very religious man, and the Quaker influence in the home was strong. The Quakers do not believe in war, and when Joseph Hewes later came to feel that a revolution in the colonies was inevitable, he left the church. Along with a changed view on religious matters, Hewes threw off other restraints imposed by the Quakers. He went to dances whenever possible, and it is said that he was also fond of the ladies.

Before the Revolution, Joseph attended school near his home and

Joseph Hewes

-later was apprenticed to a merchant in Philadelphia. When his term of apprenticeship ended, he decided to go into the mercantile business on his own. It was not long before he had made a fortune. Sometime between 1756 and 1763, Hewes moved to Edenton, North Carolina, where he established a mercantile and shipping business on the corner of Main and King Streets. He formed a partnership there with Robert Smith, a lawyer, and the firm soon owned its own wharf and sent its own ships to sea. The town of Edenton then had about 400 inhabitants.

Hewes fitted in well with the society of Edenton. He soon became engaged to Isabella Johnston, but she died shortly before the date of the wedding, and Hewes never married. Isabella was a sister of Samuel Johnston, who served as one of North Carolina's governors; after her death, Hewes continued to be a fast friend of the Johnston family.

Within three years after his arrival in Edenton, Hewes was so highly regarded that he was elected to membership in the Assembly. He served from 1766 until that body ceased meeting in 1775. When the 1773 Assembly created a Committee of Correspondence, Hewes became a member. As a member of the First Provincial Congress, he was the man who kept that body informed of the activities of the Committee in its efforts to unite the purposes and functions of the different colonies. Hewes continued to be elected a delegate each time the Provincial Congress met, and in 1774 joined the ranks of those who were sent to the Continental Congress in Philadelphia. He served in this capacity until he failed to be re-elected in 1777. He was, however, chosen a borough member of the House of Commons in 1778 and was returned to Congress the next year.

Because of his shipping interests, Hewes was well known outside North Carolina. Though it meant personal loss, when he became involved in activities leading up to the Revolutionary War, Hewes supported a policy of ceasing commercial relationships with Britain. Serving on the Committee of Marine, Hewes was responsible for fitting out vessels for the beginning of an American navy, for arranging for the construction of new ships and the acquisition of equipment, arms, and ammunition, and for the selection of officers. The knowledge of the firm of Hewes and Smith, which served as North Carolina's agent for Congress in fitting out vessels, was invaluable. Hewes had known John Paul Jones, and it was he who appointed Jones a naval officer. Hewes might well be called the first Secretary of the Navy.

Joseph Hewes served his country faithfully. On April 12, 1776, the delegates to the Provincial Congress in Halifax voted an expression of confidence in the idea of and the need for independence. Hewes was to have been a delegate at the Halifax convention, but he had not been able to leave Philadelphia in order to attend. He spent most of the year of 1776 in Philadelphia.

When the question of making a Declaration of Independence was taken before the Continental Congress at Philadelphia, some of the delegates were hestitant. The fact that Hewes himself had not originally wanted to break with Great Britain is shown in a letter he wrote to a correspondent in that country. He explained that America did not want to be independent and did not favor revolution but that Americans wanted individual freedom. At the Congress, after being convinced of the will of the people throughout the colonies, Hewes changed his opinion and signed the Declaration of Independence.

John Adams, later President of the United States, was at the Congress and has credited Hewes with turning the vote. Adams wrote, "Mr. Hewes, who had hitherto constantly voted against it, started suddenly upright, and lifting up both of his hands to Heaven, as if he had been in a trance, cried out, 'It is done! and I will abide by it.'" Thus, in this dramatic moment which John Adams recorded, was the Congress turned toward the irrevocable action.

While serving in the Continental Congress, Hewes was on the committee to prepare the Articles of Confederation. He also participated in drafting a State constitution in North Carolina. After the Provincial Congress at Halifax in November, 1776, Hewes returned to Edenton, planning to stay there until he went back to Philadelphia in February. Failing health prevented his going north.

The first Assembly under provisions of the new State Constitution met in New Bern in April, 1777. Though he was not a member, Joseph Hewes was suggested as a delegate to the Continental Congress; he received only 40 out of 90 votes. Despite this defeat, the Assembly employed Hewes to fit out two vessels; he declined, however, because he was already an agent for the Continental Congress with regard to shipping.

When the House of Commons met in 1778 and 1779, Hewes was there as a member. Delegates elected to the Continental Congress during this period included Hewes, and he returned to Philadelphia in 1779. Because of his continuing poor health, he sent his resignation to the General Assembly, which met in Halifax in October of that year, but he died before he returned home. Hewes was the only signer of the Declaration of Independence who died at the seat of government, Philadelphia. He was buried in Christ Church Cemetery in that city. Today a marker commemorates Hewes, but the site of his grave is unknown.

A tremendous and energetic worker, Hewes often applied himself to his duties 12 hours a day without stopping for food or drink. This strenuous life was probably a factor leading to the years of poor health and to his death on November 10, 1779, shortly before he reached the age of fifty.

John Penn

Moses Penn, father of Signer John Penn, was a gentleman who made money, was successful, and lived a comfortable life. Despite his achievements, he was indifferent to culture and did not think an education necessary. He allowed his son John little opportunity to attend school; in fact, John went only two or three years to a country school. Moses Penn died when his son was eighteen years old.

John Penn was born in Virginia. The dates given for his birth vary; some sources state that he was born on May 6, 1740; others say May 17, 1741. The difference probably results from the fact that the calendar has been changed since the time of Penn's birth. His mother Catherine was the daughter of John Taylor, one of the first justices of Caroline County. The Taylor family was prominent and influential.

After his father's death the son inherited a good estate. Being serious minded and realizing the need for formal education, Penn decided to study law. Edmund Pendleton, a relative who owned an excellent library, encouraged the boy by letting him use his books. Through diligence and hard work, John was able to overcome his lack of early training, and studied law on his own. Even without a teacher, Penn was able to learn enough to be admitted to the bar when he was only twenty-one years old. Two years later, July 28, 1763, he married Susannah Lyme, and they had two children, Lucy and William. After practicing law in Virginia for about 12 years, Penn decided to move to North Carolina.

The decision to come to North Carolina probably resulted from the fact that the Penns had relatives living in Granville County. This new resident very soon became a leader in the community, and in 1775 he was sent to the Provincial Congress in Hillsborough. A pleasing speaker, he won recognition from his colleagues. This popularity is shown by the fact that he was made a member of some 15 or 20 committees, most of them important ones, though the membership of the group was 184.

Within a month after his election to the Provincial Congress, Penn was chosen to succeed Richard Caswell as a delegate to the Continental Congress in Philadelphia. There he quickly lost hope of working out any satisfactory agreement with Great Britain. He wanted

John Penn

America to be free, although he would have liked for the new country and the old to live together in harmony., He served his country well during the time he was in Philadelphia, making great personal sacrifices to do so.

When North Carolina's Provincial Congress met in Halifax, April 4, 1776, Penn and the other delegates to Philadelphia were on the way home. They arrived three days later. Penn favored the resolution introduced at Halifax which empowered the delegates to the Continental Congress to "concur with the delegates of other colonies in declaring Independency, and forming foreign alliances. . . ." He returned to Philadelphia in time to join other delegates in voting for and signing the Declaration of Independence. Penn was a member of Congress until 1777, was re-elected in 1778, and served until 1780.

After the Declaration was signed, William Hooper and Joseph Hewes, the other North Carolina delegates, felt uneasy because they were afraid the masses would not be able to handle governmental responsibilities. Penn was more trustful of the people than his colleagues; he remained at his post, but he felt that the people should be made to realize the seriousness of the situation. He wrote to his friend Thomas Person, "For God's sake, my Good Sir, encourage our People, animate them to dare even to die for their country." He continued to serve efficiently. The delegates not only performed legislative duties; they had to act as financial and purchasing agents, as reporters of happenings in the country, and as the responsible officials to tie the remote colony to the life of the new nation.

The national government had no currency, no organized army, no supplies. As one person wrote, the delegates had many responsibilities and had to buy all kinds of supplies, "pamphlets, sermons, cannon, gunpowder, drums and pills." The work was so difficult that many resigned. William Hooper took that course; Joseph Hewes died; Penn was left the sole member of the three who signed the Declaration of Independence for North Carolina. Part of the extra responsibility resulted from Penn's membership on the Board of War, an agency created and given responsibility for the control of military affairs within the State. This Board was organized in Hillsborough in September, 1780. Because the other members were not active, Penn had to do the major portion of the work.

The Board of War was unpopular with the Army and with Governor Abner Nash. The Governor felt that the Board had curtailed some of his powers. As a consequence of the dissatisfaction, the Board was abolished in 1781.

In 1777, Penn had turned down a judgeship because he questioned the legality of the court. After the Revolution, he was appointed by

Robert Morris as a receiver of taxes in North Carolina for the Confederation, but he held the position for only a few weeks. In addition to these services, Penn had, along with John Williams and Cornelius Harnett, ratified the Articles of Confederation for North Carolina.

After the termination of his public career, Penn retired to the practice of law, but little is known about the remainder of his life.

Penn was an amiable and discreet man who worked with efficiency and judgment. Only one episode of his life indicates trouble with a fellow congressman. It seems that the President of Congress, Henry Laurens of South Carolina, and Penn became involved in some personal difficulty. As a result, Laurens challenged Penn to a duel. Arrangements were made for the duel, but both men boarded at the same place. The morning of the duel they ate breakfast together and then started out to go to the duel site, a vacant lot opposite the Masonic Hall on Chestnut Street in Philadelphia. On the way the men had to cross a deep slough at Fifth Street. Penn offered to help the older man across; Laurens accepted the aid. Penn then suggested that they abandon their foolish plan to duel, and Laurens agreed to forget their differences.

John Penn's character, his energy, his keen mind, and his loyalty were all used for the benefit of North Carolina and the new nation. He died in Granville County on September 14, 1788. John Penn was buried near Island Creek, but his remains were moved to Guilford Courthouse National Military Park in 1894.

William Hooper

North Carolina has been fortunate in having many men of exceptional ability and character move into its boundaries. One of these was William Hooper. A native of Boston, Massachusetts, William was born on June 17, 1742, the first child of William and Mary Hooper. His father, the rector of Trinity Church in Boston, hoped that his son would also be a minister. He wanted William to have the best possible education and he placed the boy under the tutelage of John Lovel, a famous teacher; he next sent his son to Boston Latin School for preparatory education. From there William went to Harvard College, where he entered the sophomore class because of his exceptionally good scholarship. He graduated, receiving an A.B. degree, in 1760.

Despite his father's wishes, Hooper did not feel inclined to study for the ministry. Deciding on the legal profession, the young college graduate began the study of law under James Otis, a lawyer of great prominence. Otis was a man who had advanced and liberal ideas, and it is likely that his thinking had a profound influence on Hooper. When he completed his studies, Hooper began to think about a place to settle; the Boston bar was crowded, and he decided that he would do well to move elsewhere to practice law. Having relatives in North Carolina, Hooper decided to go to Wilmington and in 1764 he left Boston. He practiced law there for a year and then went back to Boston, but his stay in Massachusetts was short. In 1765 he visited North Carolina, but two years later his father died and he returned to Boston. He had decided, by that time, to live permanently in North Carolina since he had found in his adopted State an atmosphere congenial to his liberal philosophy. Being a person of great charm and brilliance, Hooper quickly found his niche in the North Carolina community to which he moved.

In 1767 Hooper married Ann Clark, the daughter of one of the early settlers of Wilmington.

The practice of law was difficult during the years in which Hooper was active. It was necessary for lawyers to travel miles, going from court to court on horseback. Hooper often traveled as far as 180 miles from home, and he distinguished himself in all the courts in which he practiced.

Hooper served as deputy attorney-general; in that office, he performed duties which caused the Regulators to dislike him. As a result of this attitude, and because of rough treatment which Hooper suffered at the hands of the group, he became a member of Governor Tryon's military expedition against the band. The assemblies which met before 1771 had tried to relieve the Regulators of their grievances, and even after the battle, certain measures were proposed. The result was, however, a sharp clash between Governor Josiah Martin and the Assembly, with the Assembly being dissolved. A new group was chosen, and Hooper was one of those elected. He served from 1773 until the royal government was overthrown.

When a question concerning the court system was brought before the Assembly, Hooper joined the patriots in resisting British demands with regard to a matter which would have favored British subjects as against creditors living in the new country. In this and other matters, Hooper joined the patriots, feeling that many acts of the British government were harmful to the people. Because of his position and his action, Hooper achieved a place of leadership and was soon placed on the Committee of Correspondence. He presided at a meeting which resulted in the appointment of a committee to call the First Provincial Congress, and Hooper himself was elected to all five of these congresses. He was active as a leader in the first four.

William Hooper

The First Provincial Congress elected Hooper as a delegate to the Continental Congress, and he remained a member of that body until 1777. He took an active part in the debates and served on important committees. When the vote was cast for independence in 1776, Hooper was absent, but he returned in time to sign the Declaration of Independence for North Carolina.

Later this same year, the Constitutional Convention met at Halifax to set up the government for the new State. William Hooper followed these proceedings with great interest and remarked that the office of the governor had been stripped of all its former prerogatives except, as he slyly added, "the power to sign a receipt for his salary."

On April 29, 1777, William Hooper resigned from Congress and retired to his home on Masonboro Sound about eight miles from Wilmington. His public service had prevented him from practicing law regularly, and he felt it necessary to restore his fortune. During this period, however, he was again elected to office, serving in the House of Commons from 1777 to 1782.

Hooper and his family were threatened with danger during the Revolution. In January, 1781, a British force arrived at the Cape Fear River, and the Hoopers were forced to leave their home. For a time Hooper and his family were separated, but they were reunited after the enemy evacuated the city. During this turmoil Hooper lost much of his property and he also became seriously ill with malaria. In 1782 he moved to Hillsborough, where he became known as a distinguished member of the bar. During the period of residence in Hillsborough, this leader served in the House of Commons again. He favored treating the Loyalists with consideration and opposed the increased power being assumed by the common people. Defeated in his efforts to become a delegate to the Hillsborough convention, Hooper, nevertheless, favored the new Constitution and lived to see it ratified.

Never popular with the masses, William Hooper was a cultivated and distinguished gentleman. He was aloof in the eyes of many of his associates. The fact that he was a devout man is known since he introduced a resolution in Congress in 1775 calling for "public humiliation, fasting and prayer throughout the land."

In his forty-ninth year, William Hooper died, leaving a widow, two sons, and a daughter. He was buried in Hillsborough, but many years later, in 1894, his body was moved to Guilford Courthouse National Military Park, where he and John Penn share a monument, honoring them for their service to North Carolina.

Activities Following the Adoption of the Declaration

The delegates signed the Declaration of Independence on July 4, 1776, but it was not until July 22 that the news reached the North Carolina Council of Safety, which was meeting at Halifax. A resolution was adopted there declaring that the people no longer owned allegiance to Britain. The document was first publicly read to a large group at Halifax on August 1.

Meanwhile, after the adoption of the Halifax Resolves, the Provincial Congress of North Carolina had taken steps to have a constitution drafted. Upon their return from Philadelphia, Hooper and Hewes were added to a committee to work on the draft. An outline was submitted on April 25, but the Congress voted not to adopt a State constitution at that time. Nine members were selected to form a temporary government until the end of the next congress. On May 10 the Continental Congress authorized the States to draft constitutions, but North Carolina had already taken its action before receiving this word. The Council of Safety was given authority to act on behalf of the people of the colony. The Council, a permanent body, therefore became the governing body of North Carolina; Cornelius Harnett, the President, was virtually the same as Governor of North Carolina.

The Provincial Congress had adjourned on May 15, 1776. After the adoption of the Declaration of Independence and the action taken in

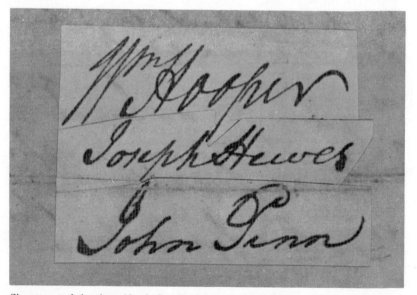

Signatures of the three North Carolina signers of the Declaration of Independence.

Philadelphia, the Council of Safety decided to order an election for delegates to the Fifth Provincial Congress. The voters were told that the body would write a constitution for the State.

The campaign was an exciting one, with the Conservative Whigs wanting few changes from the old royal form of government and the Radicals wanting simplicity in a democratic form of government. Each group won approximately the same number of delegates. The Conservatives were led by Samuel Johnston, James Iredell, William Hooper, and Archibald Maclaine. The Radicals were led by Willie Jones, Thomas Person, and Griffith Rutherford. The men who held the moderate point of view held the balance of power. The Congress met at Halifax on November 12, 1776, with 79 of the 169 delegates present. Another 70 attended before the end of the session in December. Richard Caswell was chosen President. A committee was appointed to draw up a bill of rights and a constitution. By December 17 the Declaration of Rights had been adopted and by the following day the Constitution had been approved. Both were ordered printed and distributed throughout the State; the voters were not given an opportunity to pass judgment on the documents.

The Bill of Rights listed the rights of the people against government. The Constitution of 1776 stressed popular sovereignty, included the concept of separation of powers of government, and provided for separate branches of government. There was to be an annual election by the General Assembly of delegates to the Continental Congress.

Before its adjournment on December 18, 1776, the Provincial Congress appointed Richard Caswell as Governor. He and other officials took the oath of office in January, 1777. The first General Assembly of the independent State convened on April 7, meeting in New Bern.

Various weaknesses in the new governmental structure were revealed as the State attempted to carry out normal functions as well as military activities of the Revolution. Dissension increased with the years, and divisions were shown in many ways. In 1777, when delegates were elected for the Continental Congress, the controversies were evident. John Penn defeated Joseph Hewes, who had signed the Declaration of Independence. William Hooper barely won; he refused to serve. In all phases of the State's government, the differences were revealed.

North Carolina suffered greatly during the Revolution, with military and economic pressures on all sides, and her governmental problems did not lessen as the years passed. By 1781, however, the end of war was in sight; Cornwallis surrendered at Yorktown on October 19 of that year. The period from the time of the surrender until the adoption of the United States Constitution in 1789 was critical—

North Carolina resolution regarding the reading and proclaiming of the Declaration of Independence.

both for North Carolina and for her sister States. Personal feelings entered into political endeavors; sectional interests also played a major part. The Conservatives and the Radicals remained the two chief groups.

Articles of Confederation

The relation of North Carolina to the federal government continued to be one of the greatest problems confronting the citizens. On November 15, 1777, the Continental Congress adopted the Articles of Confederation and sent the document to the States to be ratified. The North Carolina delegates to the Congress, John Penn, Cornelius Harnett, and Thomas Burke, were divided in their reaction. The former two favored the Articles and Burke opposed them, but the General Assembly ratified the document on April 24, 1778. The North

Carolina delegates tended to favor the rights of individual States as opposed to power of a centralized government. The government under the Articles of Confederation lasted from 1781 until 1789, and though much was accomplished during these years, defects and difficulties of operation under the plan of government soon became evident. Complaints increased, and plans were made for a convention which would discuss and consider the future of the new country.

Federal Convention

The North Carolina General Assembly elected delegates to attend the Federal Convention in Philadelphia. William R. Davie and Richard Dobbs Spaight were chosen from the Conservative element; Governor Richard Caswell and Alexander Martin represented the Moderate group; and Willie Jones, the Radical, was elected but refused to serve. Hugh Williamson was then chosen in his place. Caswell had to decline because of ill health, and he selected William Blount to replace him in the delegation.

Thus Davie, Martin, Spaight, Williamson, and Blount represented North Carolina in the Convention which drafted the new Constitution for the United States. The first two men named served as delegates but did not actually sign the document for the State; the latter three were the actual signers.

What kind of men were these chosen five? They were from the upper class, socially and economically; they were well educated for their day; they were successful men in their chosen careers. A brief sketch will readily show the talents each had which enabled him to play a significant role in the formation of the new government.

Alexander Martin

Alexander Martin

Alexander Martin was born in 1740, the son of Hugh and Jane Martin of Hunterdon County, New Jersey. He attended college in New Jersey and received an A.B. degree there. Moving to Salisbury, North Carolina, soon thereafter, Martin served as justice of the peace, deputy king's attorney, and judge while he carried on his business as a merchant. Martin later moved to Guilford County, which he represented in the House of Commons (1773-1774) and in the Second and Third Provincial Congresses. An active participant in military campaigns in both North Carolina and South Carolina, being a lieutenant colonel of the Second North Carolina Continental Regiment, he was later promoted to the rank of colonel. In 1777 he joined Washington's army but was arrested for cowardice at Germantown. Though acquitted in a court martial trial, Martin resigned his command and returned to North Carolina.

In 1778-1782, 1785, and 1787-1788, Martin represented Guilford County in the Senate and was speaker of several sessions. During the Revolution the politician served his country in a number of capacities and acted as Governor in the autumn and winter of 1781-1782 during the captivity of Governor Thomas Burke. In 1782 the General Assembly chose him as the new Governor over Samuel Johnston, the Conservative, and again in 1783 and 1784 over Richard Caswell. In December, 1786, he was elected to the Continental Congress where he served until the next year. A delegate to the Federal Convention in 1787, he left Philadelphia late in August before signing the completed Constitution. Though defeated in an election of delegates to the Hillsborough Convention in 1788, he was again elected Governor in 1789; in 1792 he completed the constitutional limit of three consecutive terms.

During his last term in office, Martin led the Assembly in its efforts to settle on a permanent location for the seat of government for the State. He constantly chided the legislators for their inaction in this matter, and he managed to keep free of the various quarreling towns which wanted to be chosen. Finally, in 1792, a plot of farm land was purchased, the building was begun with Governor Martin giving the formal address, and by legislative act the new capital was named "Raleigh."

Martin won favor with the General Assembly by recognizing its importance over the governorship and by accepting its opinions. He often tried to placate both sides when a question arose among those with whom he was working. Prior to 1792 Alexander Martin was a moderate Federalist, but he later leaned toward Republicanism and was elected by the 1792 Republican legislature to the United States Senate. Not being re-elected in late 1798, Martin returned to his plantation in Rockingham County. The 1790 census reported that he owned 47 slaves. Rockingham County elected him as its representative in the State Senate, 1804-1805, and being an excellent parliamentarian, he served as speaker in 1805. A trustee of several institutions, Martin was a public-spirited citizen of North Carolina for many years.

President George Washington toured the South in 1791, and when he was in Rockingham County he stayed at Martin's plantation, "Danbury." Alexander Martin never married; during his later years, his mother lived with him. He died November 2, 1807, and his mother died four days later at the age of ninety. It is said that he was buried in a "beautiful vault overlooking Dan river," that rising waters forced the casket's removal, and that the location of the grave was lost.

William Richardson Davie

Another man who attended the Constitutional Convention but who did not actually sign the document was William Richardson Davie, a native of Cumberlandshire, England. Seven years after his birth, which occurred on June 20, 1756, he was taken by his father, Archibald Davie, to the Waxhaw settlement in South Carolina. His maternal uncle, William Richardson, a childless Presbyterian clergyman, adopted and educated him. The young man attended Queens Museum in Charlotte and later Princeton, from which he graduated with honors in 1776. Davie then undertook the study of law in Salisbury and was licensed to practice in 1780, but his legal career was delayed because of war. He helped raise a troop of cavalry near Salisbury and received various commissions on to the rank of major. His military career was a notable one, and Davie contributed much to the cause of freedom through his activities. The patriot served in many capacities, and he finally was appointed commissary-general for the Carolina campaign by the North Carolina Board of War on January 6, 1781. He succeeded in feeding General Nathanael Greene's army and the State militia despite a lack of funds, but he disliked the work and resented criticism. He stayed in office until the position was discontinued and his accounts were fully made up.

After the War, in 1782, Davie settled at Halifax. There he married Sarah Jones, daughter of his old commander and a niece of Willie Jones. The couple had six children.

For 15 years Davie rode the circuits, as was then the custom, and

William Richardson Davie

went from court to court as a practicing lawyer. He appeared in nearly all important civil cases and for the defense in many criminal cases. As a representative of Halifax in the legislature almost continuously from 1786 to 1798, he became one of the leaders in North Carolina's political life. Davie was one of those chiefly responsible for the establishment of the University of North Carolina at Chapel Hill. It was he who laid the first two cornerstones of the University, acting in his capacity as Grand Master of the Masons. The University awarded Davie its first honorary degree.

William Richardson Davie was one of the delegates to the Philadelphia Convention which framed the United States Constitution. He was also a member of the Hillsborough Convention which considered the ratification of the Constitution; he urged its adoption, but to no avail. He joined others in working hard for the acceptance of the document which was ratified at the Fayetteville Convention in 1789.

On December 4, 1798, William Richardson Davie was elected Governor, but the following June he was selected by President John Adams as a commissioner to make a treaty with France. He resigned his office as Governor and left for France on the frigate "United States" from Newport. The commissioners left on November 3 and the following April 8 they were received by the French. A treaty was signed and Davie returned home, leaving Europe at the end of September, 1800.

Davie's wife having died, the widower decided to move from Halifax and devote himself to private business. He went to South Carolina in 1805. The remainder of his life was spent in looking after his personal affairs. He died on November 18, 1820, leaving three daughters and three sons.

Hugh Williamson

One of the most versatile delegates to the Federal Convention was Hugh Williamson. A theologian, a doctor, a scientist, a writer, a businessman, and a statesman, Williamson displayed competence in a variety of fields.

Hugh Williamson was born December 5, 1735, at West Nottingham, Pennsylvania. His parents were natives of Ireland. John W. Williamson, his father, was a clothier who had come to America about 1730. His mother had been brought to America as an infant, and she had had the unusual experience of having been captured by the pirate Blackbeard. Both parents were industrious, and Williamson was brought up in an atmosphere of thrift. Hugh was the oldest child of a large family, and plans were made for him to enter the ministry. His preparation for college was made at New London Cross Roads and at Newark, Delaware. A member of the first class of the College of Philadelphia, later the University of Pennsylvania, Williamson received an A.B. degree in 1757. During his student days, he taught in both the Latin and English schools.

For two years Williamson was involved in settling his father's estate, and then, in 1759, he went to Connecticut to study theology. Though never ordained, he was licensed and did preach for about two years. Becoming disgusted with various doctrinal controversies in the Presbyterian church, and having poor health, Williamson decided to change his vocation. Because of the special aptitude he had shown during his student days, the young preacher decided to accept a position as professor of mathematics at the College of Philadelphia, which place he held about three years.

During the time he was teaching mathematics, Williamson began the study of medicine, a course which he pursued full time when he went to Europe in 1764. He entered the University of Edinburgh and later studied medicine in London and Utrecht, receiving his M.D. degree from the latter institution. Returning to his home country, the young doctor settled in Philadelphia with the intention of practicing medicine there. Because of his frail physical condition, he was subject to fever when he had a patient with a serious illness. Having been fascinated by business affairs, Dr. Williamson decided to enter the mercantile business, but his great interest in scientific matters continued. On January 19, 1768, he was elected to membership in the American Philosophical Society, and the next year, Williamson was appointed a commissioner to study the transit of the planets Venus on June 3, 1769, and Mercury, on November 9, 1769. As a result of studies of comets, he published "An Essay on Comets," in the first volume of *Transaction of the American Philosophical Society*. His publication won him such widespread recognition that the University of Leyden awarded him the LL.D. degree. While in Europe in the 1770's, Williamson's interest in science continued. He read a paper, published in 1775, on the electric eel.

An example of Williamson's devotion to education is shown by his activities in support of an academy in Newark, Delaware. As a trustee of that institution, he toured the West Indies to obtain subscriptions; the next year, 1773, he undertook another trip of a similar nature, this time to Europe. While he was waiting for his ship to sail, he was a witness to the Boston Tea Party and carried the first news of

Hugh Williamson

this event to England. When he reached that country, Williamson was called to testify before the Privy Council; he predicted that there would be revolt in the colonies if the British policies were not changed. Shortly before he left England, he was able to obtain letters from Massachusetts which, when published, tended to widen the breach between the mother country and the colonies. Williamson delivered these letters to Benjamin Franklin, and the two men became close friends and worked together carrying out numerous experiments.

During his stay abroad, Williamson wrote a letter to Lord Mansfield, called *The Plea of the Colonies*. This appeared anonymously in 1775, and it answered charges which had been made against the colonies concerning disloyalty and unrest. The letter was written in the hope that it would help the cause of friendship, but efforts of this kind were too late, for the colonies were already on the verge of rebellion. Williamson was in Holland when he heard of the Declaration of Independence. In December, 1776, he sailed for America, but the ship was captured off Delaware. Williamson managed to escape in a small boat, and he arrived back in his native country March 15, 1777.

With his medical training, it would have been logical for Williamson to have entered the service of his country during the Revolutionary War. He found, however, that the medical positions of interest were filled, and this situation led him to decide to go into business. He and his brother went into the mercantile business, first in Charleston, South Carolina, and then in Edenton. A large trade with the West Indies was built up. Though his primary interest was his business, Williamson also engaged in the practice of medicine; he offered his services to Governor Caswell and was later made surgeon-general of State troops. It was Williamson who was sent to New Bern to vaccinate troops against smallpox. He was present at the Battle of Camden and crossed British lines often to treat American soldiers who were prisoners of war. The British, who had confidence in him, also used his services.

Williamson was a pioneer in advocating the use of inoculation against diseases. He felt that this prevention was necessary before there could be effective military service. He carried out experiments to determine the relation of diet, shelter, clothing, drainage, and other factors to illness. During the time they were under Williamson's care, out of a force which ranged from 500 to 1,200 men, only two died during a period of six months. This was a very unusual record for this day.

At the end of the Revolutionary period, Williamson entered the political life of North Carolina. He represented Edenton in the House of Commons in 1782; the same year he was elected a delegate to the Continental Congress in Philadelphia. He served in that body until 1785; that year, he again went to the House of Commons as a representative from Chowan County. Governor Caswell appointed Williamson to succeed Willie Jones, and in 1787 he returned to the Philadelphia Convention, remaining a member until that body went out of existence. He was an apt debater, though a poor orator. His writings were on many topics, including the evils of paper money. An excise tax was favored by him in lieu of a land or poll tax. He supported the adoption of domestic manufactures, and his publications reveal a great deal about the commercial and economic life of the United States and North Carolina during the late eighteenth century.

Williamson was an active delegate, speaking more often and serving on more committees than any delegate from North Carolina. He favored a plural executive, and he thought that the legislative branch of the government should elect the executive. After signing the new Constitution, the delegate came home and worked for its ratification. He published articles in the North Carolina newspapers explaining its provisions. Though not a member of the Hillsborough Convention of 1788, which failed to ratify the Constitution, Williamson was present at the Fayetteville Convention of 1789 and voted for its ratification.

Williamson served as the agent of the State to settle its accounts with the federal government. The next year, 1789, he was elected a member of the first Congress of the United States; he was also a member of the second session. When his term expired in 1793, he moved to the home of his wife, Maria Apthorpe, daughter of a wealthy New York merchant, whom he had married in 1789. The remainder of his life was spent in New York in literary and scientific pursuits. His research and writings brought him fame, and he was chosen a member of the Holland Society of Science and the Society of Arts and Sciences of Utrecht; he received an honorary degree from the University of Leyden.

Williamson's interest in education was recognized by his appointment as one of the original trustees of the University of North Carolina. He also served as a trustee of the College of Physicians and Surgeons and of the University of the State of New York and a founder of the Literary and Philosophical Society of New York and a leading member of the New-York Historical Society.

Williamson published a history of North Carolina in 1812. His study on climate, which had been published a year earlier, was used as an introduction to the history. A great deal of work went into the history, but lack of availability of records resulted in failure. Because of his reputation in other fields, the history received more recognition than it would have otherwise, but Williamson lacked ability as a historian.

During the last years of his life, Williamson was saddened by the death of his wife and his two sons. Though his own health was poor, death was sudden. He died while driving in his carriage, May 22, 1819, in New York City.

Hugh Williamson was a brilliant and significant leader of North Carolina. His name is one which should be remembered by citizens today, for his many endeavors had a profound and lasting effect on the history of the State.

William Blount

Three brothers—Thomas, John Gray, and William Blount—were outstanding in the business and political life of North Carolina during the latter part of the eighteenth century. One of them, William, signed the Constitution on behalf of the State.

William Blount was born March 26, 1749, the first of eight children in his family. His father, Jacob, had married Barbara Gray in 1748. The family lived in the Pamlico Sound area of North Carolina.

William received a good education for his time. Not much is known about his youth, but both he and his father fought under Governor William Tryon at the Battle of Alamance, May 16, 1771. They both served during the Revolution as paymasters in the Continental Line. William was commissioned in the Third North Carolina Regiment on December 11, 1778. Early that same year, he married Mary Grainger (also spelled Granger), of Wilmington; they had six children who grew to adulthood.

Blount was active in the public life of North Carolina from the time of the Revolution. Between 1780 and 1789 he served in the House of Commons four times, and was Speaker of the House once, and was a Senate member twice. A delegate to the Continental Congress in 1782-1783 and 1786-1787, and a member of the Federal Convention in Philadelphia, which framed the Constitution, Blount impressed his colleagues favorably. Though he was only thirty-eight at the time, mention was made of his integrity, honesty, and sincerity. Not being noted as a speaker, Blount took almost no part in the debates. In fact, some accounts of Blount's life indicate that he was absent during most of the sessions of the Congress. He did, however, sign the Constitution and vote for its ratification in the North Carolina Convention of 1789.

William Blount

In the new national government, Blount was anxious to play an active part; he hoped to be elected to the United States Senate from North Carolina but failed in this ambition. An interest in the trans-Alleghany region, because of speculation in western lands and as a representative in dealing with the Indians, made Blount more than a mere spectator. When he learned that Congress had provided for a territorial form of government for this area, he actively and successfully sought the position as governor of this territory. President George Washington appointed Blount governor of the Territory of the United States South of the River Ohio on August 17, 1790, but he did not reach the area of Tennessee until October of that year. With the new office, Blount was also made Superintendent of Indian Affairs for the Southern Department.

Upon reaching the mountain area, Blount found that the people were divided into two factions. The frontier interests and the policy of the United States government with respect to Indians were not always in harmony. Blount handled the situation with great tact; he tried to be sympathetic with the settlers of the frontier and yet carry out orders from the government representatives in the capital. At the same time, he maintained his ability to conduct himself with political astuteness.

Because of his popularity with the settlers and with leaders of the territory, Blount was chosen president of a convention which met in January, 1796, and proclaimed that the territory would become the State of Tennessee. The first legislature of the new State elected Blount to the United States Senate, but he served there only a short time.

William Blount had continued to deal in western lands during his term as governor of the territory, and he found himself involved in financial troubles. He also became active in a scheme of certain Indians and frontier settlers to co-operate with the British fleet and attack Spanish Florida and Louisiana with the hope of transferring those territories to Great Britain. A bit of intrigue showed up when one of Blount's letters came to light. In the letter Blount spoke in carefully worded language about the plan and told of his wishes to have the Indians aid in the scheme. This letter was addressed to a Cherokee interpreter, but it fell into the hands of President John Adams. The President sent it to Congress in July, 1797. The result was like a bombshell in Philadelphia. Blount hoped that people would interpret the letter to see good in it, but the senators felt differently. A vote of that group expelled the Senator on July 8, the vote being 25 to 1 in favor of this action. Impeachment proceedings were later initiated in the House of Representatives. The impeachment trial opened on December 17, 1798, the first such trial in the history of the United States. Blount was brilliantly defended, and the question was raised as to whether or not the Senate could impeach a man already expelled. Delays prevented the conclusion of the matter from coming before the Senate for final decision until early 1799. At that time, the proceedings were dismissed for lack of jurisdiction.

While all of these actions were occurring, Blount returned to Tennessee. The people there still had confidence in him; this regard was shown by the fact that he was elected to the State Senate in 1798 and became speaker of that branch of the legislature.

William Blount might well have gone on to higher positions of leadership in Tennessee but for his death in March, 1800.

Richard Dobbs Spaight, Sr.

On a Sunday afternoon in 1802 a duel was fought in New Bern—a duel which was to end the life of one of the most prominent North Carolinians of his generation. Who was this man? Why was he important? What events led to the duel? What contributions did he make to North Carolina which rate him a place in the State's history?

The man was Richard Dobbs Spaight, Sr., a person who accomplished so much in his lifetime that it is hard to know where to begin in describing his achievements. It is significant to note that he was born in North Carolina, because he was the first native-born son to become Governor of the State. His birth occurred on March 25, 1758, in New Bern—the same town in which he later died. His parents were aristocrats, and his home was one in which he could benefit from many of the material advantages of the times. His mother, Margaret Dobbs Spaight, was a sister of Royal Governor Arthur Dobbs; his father, Richard Spaight, was a native of Ireland who had come to the colony of North Carolina with Dobbs when he became Governor. Spaight had served as a member of the colonial council and as secretary of the colony.

Richard was left an orphan before he was nine. His Uncle Arthur had also died, and the boy's guardians decided to send him abroad to school. He received his early schooling in Ireland.

In the meantime, back in New Bern, Royal Governor Tryon decided to build his Palace. Part of the site he chose was land belonging to the estate of the child, Richard Spaight. Unable to obtain the land in any other way, Tryon had it condemned and handed over to the province and thus made available for his building plans. For 30 years afterward, Richard Spaight was engaged in litigation over this seizure;

once the matter was even presented to the State legislature, with no results. Toward the close of his life, Spaight finally received some recompense for this land.

After his studies in Ireland, the young man moved to Scotland to attend the University of Glasgow. When he had finished his education, Spaight made an important decision: He decided to return to America. Considering the facts that he had had exceptionally good training, had a family background which was far from democratic, and had lived abroad during his formative years, such a decision was unusual. It was indeed fortunate for North Carolina and for the nation that Spaight made this choice, for he was destined to play a vital role in the history of his native country.

Another trip was made across the Atlantic, and the passengers landed in the midst of war. Spaight soon found himself involved in the conflict; he was present at the Battle of Camden during the Revolutionary War; and he served as aide to General Richard Caswell, commander of the State militia. Once during this time, he was in New Bern and learned that a Loyalist privateer had sneaked into the harbor. He and a friend fitted out a schooner and gave chase. A sudden storm prevented an actual engagement between the two ships, but the enemy fled and was seen no more.

Spaight's military career ended when his long record of public service began. The voters chose him to represent them in 1779 in the House of Commons, which was the name given to the lower house of the legislature in colonial days. Because of a question concerning the legality of the election, it was set aside, but this event did not prevent Spaight from being elected again and again. He represented either New Bern or Craven County every time the House met between 1781 and 1787 except for one year; he also served in 1792. His fellow lawmakers expressed their confidence in Spaight by electing him Speaker of the House of Commons in 1785. Few people have had a political career which began as early as Spaight's; he was only twenty-three years old when he first served in the General Assembly.

Exceptionally good training and experience qualified Spaight for positions of leadership and trust, not only in North Carolina but also in the nation. When first nominated to go to the Continental Congress, the members of the General Assembly decided not to make him one of the delegates, but on April 25, 1783, Governor Alexander Martin named Spaight to succeed William Blount, who had resigned. Spaight was elected the next year in his own right and served as a member of the Congress until he resigned in 1785.

Two years later the Constitutional Convention delegates assembled in Philadelphia to discuss ideas and to work out plans for the federal

Richard Dobbs Spaight, Sr.

government. Included in the delegation from North Carolina was Spaight. Though no actual business was transacted until May 25, 1787, he had arrived in Philadelphia by May 13. No doubt he made many friends and impressed others with his fine qualities during the days prior to the formal sessions. Before leaving Philadelphia, Spaight voted for the Constitution and signed it as one of North Carolina's delegates. The next year a convention was called by the General Assembly of North Carolina to meet in Hillsborough for the purpose of discussing the new Constitution and determining whether or not North Carolina would ratify it. Having been a delegate in Philadelphia, and having supported the action taken there, it was natural that Spaight should represent his home county at Hillsborough. James Iredell, a lawyer of Edenton and later a judge, led the fight for the adoption of this guide for government. He received support from Spaight and William R. Davie, who had also been at the Philadelphia sessions. Despite their efforts, North Carolina failed to ratify the Constitution at this first assembly. The next year another meeting was called; on November 21, 1789, in Fayetteville, this body ratified the Constitution. The vote was 195 in favor of ratification, 77 against. The debates of the Philadelphia Convention had been published, and probably many North Carolinians had read the record and knew of the national discussion when they met in Fayetteville to cast their votes on the issue.

Spaight was suggested for several offices during these years, but he was not always selected for the posts. For example, in November, 1787, he was nominated for Governor, but the Federalists were in power and Samuel Johnston was chosen instead. After North Carolina ratified the Constitution, the Anti-Federalists proposed his name as a candidate for United States Senator, but again he was defeated.

These decisions did not end the political career of Richard Dobbs Spaight, but a decline in his physical condition forced him to withdraw from public life for a period of time. He had lived a hard and strenuous life, traveling great distances under difficult conditions and working conscientiously as a legislator and delegate to both national and State conventions. As a result Spaight's health was so poor that he was forced to spend months in an effort to find a cure. During his four-year retirement he traveled widely, spending some time in the West Indies. Though his health was never again perfect, it did improve, and North Carolina again had his services as a public servant.

In 1792, when Spaight felt well enough to re-enter the political world, he was chosen Governor of North Carolina by the General

Assembly, a position he held until 1795 when Samuel Ashe succeeded him. During his term of office, in 1793, the Governor served as a federal elector to vote for President and Vice-President of the United States. In an effort to promote peace, Spaight issued a proclamation seeking neutrality in European wars; when he learned that several French privateers were being fitted out in Wilmington, he had the ships seized and held.

The General Assembly met in Raleigh for the first time in December, 1794, during Spaight's tenure as Governor. Plans had been made to order a new seal for the State, and an order was placed with a Philadelphia firm in the summer of 1793. Because of sickness in that city, the delivery was delayed until the next summer; when the seal was finally completed, it was sent to New Bern. To the dismay of Spaight and other State officials, the new seal was found to lack a screw, making it useless. The General Assembly, in 1795, authorized the use of the old seal of 1778 until a new one could be obtained.

Spaight was the first native-born North Carolinian to be elected to the office of Governor; he and his son Richard Dobbs Spaight, Jr., and, later, W. Kerr Scott and his son Robert W. Scott are the only examples in the history of the State of fathers and sons being elected to the office of Governor.

When he was thirty-one years old, Richard Dobbs Spaight married Mary Leach, from Philadelphia. At the time of their marriage, a Philadelphia magazine carried a notice of the wedding, commenting that the bride was "a young lady whose amiable character and beautiful person, added to an extensive fortune, promise much felicity to this worthy pair." When President George Washington traveled through the South in 1791, the people of New Bern gave a ball at the beautiful Tryon Palace, and it was Mrs. Spaight who led the minuet with the distinguished guest as her partner. Governor Spaight and his wife had three children, two sons and a daughter; both of the sons remained bachelors.

At the end of his term as Governor, Spaight moved to New Bern. He lived there for two years and then was elected to Congress. The Sixth Congress met in Philadelphia on December 2, 1799, and Spaight took the oath of office the next month. He also attended the Congress which met in Washington in November, 1800, and he cast a vote in favor of Thomas Jefferson when the House of Representatives met to break the tie between Jefferson and Burr for President. Though he generally opposed the Federalists, Spaight was not narrow in his views, and he voted independently when he thought the Federalists were right.

After serving in Congress for a little over three years, Spaight decided not to seek re-election. He did, however, return to the General Assembly of North Carolina, becoming a State Senator in 1802. Unfortunately, the campaign was a bitter one and the results of events occurring during this time cost Spaight his life.

A man named John Stanly, a Federalist and a lawyer from New Bern, succeeded Spaight in Congress. Stanly accused Spaight of opposing legislation which he thought should have been supported for the good of North Carolina and for dodging important matters while in Congress, pleading poor health as an excuse. Spaight ignored the charges until after he had been re-elected to the General Assembly and then he had handbills printed and distributed. In these, he replied to Stanly's accusations.

During this period of the country's history, duels were the accepted way of settling bitter arguments. Because of the heated feelings resulting from their differences, a challenge to a duel was passed and accepted. The two men met on the outskirts of New Bern about 5:30 on Sunday afternoon, September 5, 1802. On the fourth fire, Spaight was wounded in the right side; he died the next day, about 23 hours after the duel had taken place. Spaight was buried on September 7, 1802, near New Bern.

Criminal proceedings were brought against Stanly, but he asked for pardon, which was granted. Stanly later attained positions of honor and trust before his death in 1834.

Richard Dobbs Spaight died at the age of forty-four. He accomplished far more in his lifetime than most people, and North Carolinians should honor this early leader who helped bring about independence and a strong government for both the United States and his native State.

APPENDIX I

THE DECLARATION OF INDEPENDENCE

(Unanimously Adopted in Congress, July 4, 1776, at Philadelphia)

When, in the course of human events, it becomes necessary for one people to dissolve the political bands which have connected them with another, and to assume among the powers of the earth, the separate and equal station to which the Laws of Nature and of Nature's God entitles them, a decent respect to the opinions of mankind requires that they should declare the causes which impel them to the separation.

We hold these truths to be self-evident: That all men are created equal; that they are endowed by their Creator with certain inalienable Rights; that among these are Life, Liberty and the pursuit of Happiness. That, to secure these rights, Governments are instituted among Men, deriving their just powers from the consent of the governed; That, whenever any Form of Government becomes destructive of these ends, it is the Right of the People to alter or to abolish it, and to institute new Government, laying its foundations on such principles, and organizing its powers in such forms, as to them shall seem most likely to effect their Safety and Happiness. Prudence, indeed, will dictate that Governments long established should not be changed for light and transient causes; and, accordingly, all experience hath shewn, that mankind are more disposed to suffer, while evils are sufferable, than to right themselves by abolishing the forms to which they are accustomed. But when a long train of abuses and usurpations, pursuing invariably the same Object, evidences a design to reduce them under absolute Despotism, it is their right, it is their duty, to throw off such Government, and to provide new Guards for their future security. Such has been the patient sufferance of these Colonies, and such is now the necessity which constrains them to alter their former Systems of Government. The history of the present King of Great Britain is a history of repeated injuries and usurpations, all having in direct object the establishment of an absolute Tyranny over these States. To prove this, let Facts be submitted to a candid world.

He has refused his assent to Laws, the most wholesome and necessary for the public good.

He has forbidden his Governors to pass Laws of immediate and pressing importance, unless suspended in their operation till his Assent should be obtained; and, when so suspended, he has utterly neglected to attend to them.

He has refused to pass other Laws for the accommodation of large districts of people, unless those people would relinquish the right of Representation in the Legislature—a right inestimable to them, and formidable to tyrants only.

He has called together legislative bodies at places unusual, uncomfortable and distant from the depository of their public Records, for the sole purpose of fatiguing them into compliance with his measures.

He has dissolved Representative Houses repeatedly, for opposing with manly firmness his invasions on the rights of the people.

He has refused for a long time, after such dissolutions, to cause others to be elected; whereby the Legislative powers, incapable of Annihilation, have returned to the People at large for their exercise; the State remaining, in the meantime, exposed to all the dangers of invasion from without, and convulsions within.

He has endeavored to prevent the population of these States for that purpose obstructing the Laws of Naturalization of Foreigners; refusing to pass others to encourage their migration hither, and raising the conditions of new Appropriations of Lands.

He has obstructed the Administration of Justice, by refusing his assent to laws for establishing Judiciary Powers.

He has made Judges dependent on his Will alone, for the tenure of their offices, and the amount and payment of their salaries.

He has erected a multitude of New Offices, and sent hither swarms of Officers to harass our people, and eat out their substance.

He has kept among us, in times of peace, Standing Armies without the Consent of Our Legislature.

He has affected to render the Military independent of, and superior to, the Civil power.

He has combined with others to subject us to a jurisdiction foreign to our constitution, and unacknowledged by our laws; giving his Assent to their Acts of pretended Legislation:

For quartering large bodies of armed troops among us:

For protecting them, by a mock Trial, from punishment for any Murders which they should commit on the inhabitants of these States:

For cutting off our Trade with all parts of the world:

For imposing Taxes on us without our Consent:

For depriving us, in many cases, of the benefits of Trial by jury:

For transporting us beyond Seas, to be tried for pretended offenses:

For abolishing the free System of English Laws in a neighboring Province, establishing therein an Arbitrary government, and enlarging its Boundaries, so as to render it at once an example and fit instrument for introducing the same absolute rule into these Colonies:

For taking away our Charters, abolishing our most valuable Laws, and altering fundamentally, the Forms of our Governments:

For suspending our own Legislatures, and declaring themselves invested with power to legislate for us in all cases whatsoever.

He has abdicated Government here, by declaring us out of his Protection and waging War against us.

He has plundered our seas, ravaged our Coasts, burnt our towns, and destroyed the lives of our people.

He is at this time transporting large Armies of foreign mercenaries to complete the works of death, desolation and tyranny, already begun with circumstances of Cruelty and perfidy scarcely paralleled in the most barbarous ages, and totally unworthy the Head of a civilized nation.

He has constrained our fellow-Citizens, taken captive on the high Seas, to bear Arms against their Country, to become the executioners of their friends and Brethren, or to fall themselves by their Hands.

He has excited domestic insurrections amongst us, and has endeavored to bring on the inhabitants of our frontiers, the merciless Indian Savages, whose known rule of warfare is an undistinguished destruction of all ages, sexes, and conditions.

In every stage of these Oppressions We have Petitioned for Redress in the most humble terms; Our repeated Petitions have been answered only by repeated injury. A Prince, whose character is thus marked by every act which may define a Tyrant, is unfit to be the ruler of a free people.

Nor have we been wanting in attention to our British brethren. We have warned them from time to time of attempts by their legislature to extend an unwarrantable jurisdiction over us. We have reminded them of the circumstances of our emigration and settlement here. We have appealed to their native justice and magnanimity, and we have conjured them by the ties of our common kindred to disavow these usurpations, which inevitably interrupt our connections with correspondence. They, too, have been deaf to the voice of justice and of consanguinity. We must, therefore, acquiesce in the necessity, which denounces our Separation, and hold them, as we hold the rest of mankind—Enemies in War, in Peace Friends.

WE, THEREFORE, the Representatives of the United States of America, in General Congress Assembled; appealing to the Supreme Judge of the world for the rectitude of our intentions, do, in the Name and by authority of the good People of these Colonies, solemnly publish and declare, That these United Colonies are, and of Right ought to be free and independent States; that they are Absolved from All Allegiance to the British Crown, and that all political connections between them and the State of Great Britain is, and ought to be, totally dissolved; and that as Free and Independent States, they have full power to levy War, conclude Peace, contract Alliances, establish Commerce, and to do all other Acts and Things which Independent States may of right do. And for the support of this Declaration, with a firm reliance on the protection of Divine Providence, we mutually pledge to each other our Lives, our Fortunes, and our sacred Honor.

John Hancock

Button Gwinnett
Lyman Hall
Geo. Walton
Wm. Hooper
Joseph Hewes
John Penn
Thos. Stone
Charles Carroll of Carrollton
James Wilson
Geo. Ross
Caesar Rodney
Geo. Reed
Tho. M. Kean
Wm. Floyd
Phil. Livingston
Frans. Lewis
Lewis Morris
Richd. Stockton
Jno. Witherspoon
Fras. Hopkinson
John Hart
Abra Clark
George Wythe
Richard Henry Lee
Th. Jefferson
Benja. Harrison
Thos. Nelson, Jr.
Francis Lightfoot Lee

Edward Rutledge
Thomas Heyward, Junr.
Thomas Lynch, Junr.
Arthur Middleton
Samuel Chase
Wm. Paca
Carter Braxton
Robt. Morris
Benjamin Rush
Benja. Franklin
John Morton
Geo. Clymer
Jas. Smith
Geo. Taylor
Josiah Bartlett
Wm. Hipple
Saml. Adams
John Adams
Robt. Treat Payne
Eldridge Gerry
Step. Hopkins
William Ellery
Roger Sherman
Samuel Huntington
Wm. Williams
Oliver Woolcott
Matthew Thornton

APPENDIX II

THE CONSTITUTION OF THE UNITED STATES

PREAMBLE

We, the people of the United States, in order to form a more perfect Union, establish justice, insure domestic tranquility, provide for the common defense, promote the general welfare, and secure the blessings of liberty to ourselves and our posterity, do ordain and establish this Constitution for the United States of America.

ARTICLE I

SECTION 1—All legislative powers herein granted shall be vested in a Congress of the United States, which shall consist of a Senate and a House of Representatives.

SEC. 2—1. The House of Representatives shall be composed of members chosen every second year by the people of the several States, and the electors in each State shall have the qualifications requisite for electors of the most numerous branch of the State Legislature.

2. No person shall be a Representative who shall not have attained to the age of twenty-five years, and been seven years a citizen of the United States, and who shall not, when elected, be an inhabitant of that State in which he shall be chosen.

3. Representatives and direct taxes shall be apportioned among the several States which may be included within this Union, according to their respective numbers, which shall be determined by adding to the whole number of free persons, including those bound to service for a term of years and excluding Indians not taxed, three-fifths of all other persons. The actual enumeration shall be made within three years after the first meeting of the Congress of the United States, and within every subsequent term of ten years, in such manner as they shall by law direct. The number of Representatives shall not exceed one for every thirty thousand, but each State shall have at least one Representative; and until such enumeration shall be made, the State of New Hampshire shall be entitled to choose 3; Massachusetts, 8; Rhode Island and Providence Plantations, 1; Connecticut, 5; New York, 6; New Jersey, 4; Pennsylvania, 8; Delaware, 1; Maryland, 6; Virginia, 10; North Carolina, 5; South Carolina, 5; and Georgia, 3.*

4. When vacancies happen in the representation from any State the Executive Authority thereof shall issue writs of election to fill such vacancies.

5. The House of Representatives shall choose their Speaker and other officers, and shall have the sole power of impeachment.

SEC. 3—1. The Senate of the United States shall be composed of two Senators from each State, chosen by the Legislature thereof for six years; and each Senator shall have one vote.†

2. Immediately after they shall be assembled in consequence of the first election, they shall be divided as equally as may be into three classes. The seats of the Senators of the first class shall be vacated at the expiration of the second year; of the second class at the expiration of the fourth year; and of the third class at the expiration of the sixth year, so that one-third may be chosen every second year, and if vacancies happen by resignation, or otherwise, during the recess of the Legislature of any State, the Ex-

---

* See Article XIV, Amendments.
† See Article XVII, Amendments.

ecutive thereof may make temporary appointments until the next meeting of the Legislature, which shall then fill such vacancies.*

3. No person shall be a Senator who shall not have attained to the age of thirty years, and been nine years a citizen of the United States, and who shall not, when elected, be an inhabitant of that State for which he shall be chosen.

4. The Vice President of the United States shall be President of the Senate, but shall have no vote, unless they be equally divided.

5. The Senate shall choose their other officers, and also a President *pro tempore*, in the absence of the Vice President, or when he shall exercise the office of President of the United States.

6. The Senate shall have the sole power to try all impeachments. When sitting for that purpose, they shall be on oath or affirmation. When the President of the United States is tried, the Chief Justice shall preside; and no person shall be convicted without the concurrence of two-thirds of the members present.

7. Judgment in cases of impeachment shall not extend further than to removal from office, and disqualification to hold and enjoy any office of honor, trust, or profit under the United States; but the party convicted shall nevertheless be liable and subject to indictment, trial, judgment, and punishment, according to law.

SEC. 4—1. The times, places, and manner of holding elections for Senators and Representatives shall be prescribed in each State by the Legislature thereof, but the Congress may at any time by law make or alter such regulations, except as to the places of choosing Senators.

2. The Congress shall assemble at least once in every year, and such meeting shall be on the first Monday in December, unless they shall by law appoint a different day.

SEC. 5—1. Each House shall be the judge of the elections, returns, and qualifications of its own members, and a majority of each shall constitute a quorum to do business; but a smaller number may adjourn from day to day, and may be authorized to compel the attendance of absent members, in such manner and under such penalties as each House may provide.

2. Each House may determine the rules of its proceedings, punish its members for disorderly behavior, and, with the concurrence of two-thirds, expel a member.

3. Each House shall keep a journal of its proceedings, and from time to time publish the same, excepting such parts as may in their judgment require secrecy; and the yeas and nays of the members of either House on any question shall, at the desire of one-fifth of those present, be entered on the journal.

4. Neither House, during the session of Congress, shall, without the consent of the other, adjourn for more than three days, nor to any other place than that in which the two Houses shall be sitting.

SEC. 6—1. The Senators and Representatives shall receive a compensation for their services, to be ascertained by law, and paid out of the Treasury of the United States. They shall in all cases, except treason, felony, and breach of the peace, be privileged from arrest during their attendance at the session of their respective Houses, and in going to and returning from the same; and for any speech or debate in either House they shall not be questioned in any other place.

---

* See Article XVII, Amendments.

2. No Senator or Representative shall, during the time for which he was elected, be appointed to any civil office under the authority of the United States which shall have been created, or the emoluments whereof shall have been increased during such time; and no person holding any office under the United States shall be a member of either House during his continuance in office.

Sec. 7—1. All bills for raising revenue shall originate in the House of Representatives; but the Senate may propose or concur with amendments, as on other bills.

2. Every bill which shall have passed the House of Representatives and the Senate shall, before it becomes a law, be presented to the President of the United States; if he approves, he shall sign it, but if not, he shall return it, with his objections, to that House in which it shall have originated, who shall enter the objections at large on their journal, and proceed to reconsider it. If after such reconsideration two-thirds of that House shall agree to pass the bill, it shall be sent together with the objections, to the other House, by which it shall likewise be reconsidered, and if approved by two-thirds of that House, it shall become a law. But in all such cases the votes of both Houses shall be determined by yeas and nays, and the names of the persons voting for and against the bill shall be entered on the journal of each House respectively. If any bill shall not be returned by the President within ten days (Sundays excepted) after it shall have been presented to him, the same shall be a law, in like manner as if he had signed it, unless the Congress by their adjournment prevent its return, in which case it shall not be a law.

3. Every order, resolution, or vote to which the concurrence of the Senate and House of Representatives may be necessary (except on a question of adjournment) shall be presented to the President of the United States; and before the same shall take effect, shall be approved by him, or being disapproved by him, shall be repassed by two-thirds of the Senate and House of Representatives, according to the rules and limitations prescribed in the case of a bill.

Sec. 8. The Congress shall have power:

1. To lay and collect taxes, duties, imposts and excises, to pay the debts and provide for the common defense and general welfare of the United States; but all duties, imposts and excises shall be uniform throughout the United States;

2. To borrow money on the credit of the United States;

3. To regulate commerce with foreign nations, and among the several States, and with the Indian tribes;

4. To establish a uniform rule of naturalization, and uniform laws on the subject of bankruptcies throughout the United States;

5. To coin money, regulate the value thereof, and of foreign coin, and fix the standards of weights and measures;

6. To provide for the punishment of counterfeiting the securities and current coins of the United States;

7. To establish postoffices and postroads;

8. To promote the progress of science and useful arts, by securing, for limited times, to authors and inventors, the exclusive right to their respective writings and discoveries;

9. To constitute tribunals inferior to the Supreme Court;

10. To define and punish piracies and felonies committed on the high seas, and offenses against the law of nations;

11. To declare war, grant letters of marque and reprisal, and make rules concerning captures on land and water;

12. To raise and support armies, but no appropriation of money to that use shall be for a longer term than two years;

13. To provide and maintain a navy;

14. To make rules for the government and regulation of the land and naval forces;

15. To provide for calling for the militia to execute the laws of the Union, suppress insurrections, and repel invasions;

16. To provide for organizing, arming, and disciplining the militia, and for governing such part of them as may be employed in the service of the United States, reserving to the States respectively the appointment of the officers and the authority of training the militia according to the discipline prescribed by Congress;

17. To exercise exclusive legislation in all cases whatsoever over such district (not exceeding ten miles square) as may by cession of particular States and the acceptance of Congress, become the seat of Government of the United States, and to exercise like authority over all places purchased by the consent of the Legislature of the State in which the same shall be, for the erection of forts, magazines, arsenals, dock-yards, and other needful buildings;—and

18. To make all laws which shall be necessary and proper for carrying into execution the foregoing powers, and all other powers vested by this Constitution in the Government of the United States or any department or officer thereof.

SEC. 9—1. The migration or importation of such persons as any of the States now existing shall think proper to admit, shall not be prohibited by the Congress prior to the year one thousand eight hundred and eight, but a tax or duty may be imposed on such importations, not exceeding ten dollars for each person.

2. The privilege of the writ of *habeas corpus* shall not be suspended, unless when in cases of rebellion or invasion the public safety may require it.

3. No bill of attainder or *ex post facto* law shall be passed.

4. No capitation or other direct tax shall be laid, unless in proportion to the census or enumeration hereinbefore directed to be taken.*

5. No tax or duty shall be laid on articles exported from any State.

6. No preference shall be given by any regulation of commerce or revenue to the ports of one State over those of another; nor shall vessels bound to, or from, one State be obliged to enter, clear, or pay duties in another.

7. No money shall be drawn from the Treasury but in consequence of appropriations made by law; and a regular statement and account of the receipts and expenditures of all public money shall be published from time to time.

8. No title of nobility shall be granted by the United States; and no person holding any office of profit or trust under them, shall, without the consent of the Congress, accept of any present, emolument, office, or title, of any kind whatever, from any king, prince, or foreign state.

---

* See Article XVI, Amendments.

Sec. 10—1. No State shall enter into any treaty, alliance, or confederation; grant letters of marque and reprisal; coin money; emit bills of credit; make anything but gold and silver coin a tender in payment of debts; pass any bill of attainder; *ex post facto* law, or law impairing the obligation of contracts, or grant any title of nobility.

2. No State shall, without the consent of the Congress, lay any imposts or duties on imports or exports except what may be absolutely necessary for executing its inspection laws; and the net produce on all duties and imports, laid by any State on imports or exports, shall be for the use of the Treasury of the United States; and all such laws shall be subject to the revision and control of the Congress.

3. No State shall, without the consent of Congress, lay any duty of tonnage, keep troops, or ships of war in time of peace, enter into any agreement or compact with another State, or with a foreign power, or engage in war, unless actually invaded, or in such imminent danger as will not admit delay.

ARTICLE II

Section 1—1. The executive power shall be vested in a President of the United States of America. He shall hold his office during the term of four years, and, together with the Vice President, chosen for the same term, be elected as follows:

2. Each State shall appoint, in such manner as the legislature thereof may direct, a number of electors, equal to the whole number of Senators and Representatives to which the State may be entitled in the Congress; but no Senator or Representative or person holding an office of trust or profit under the United States shall be appointed an elector.

3. The electors shall meet in their respective States, and vote by ballot for two persons, of whom one at least shall not be an inhabitant of the same state with themselves. And they shall make a list of all the persons voted for, and of the number of votes for each; which list they shall sign and certify, and transmit, sealed, to the seat of the Government of the United States, directed to the President of the Senate. The President of the Senate shall, in the presence of the Senate and House of Representatives open all the certificates, and the votes shall be counted. The person having the greatest number of votes shall be the President, if such number be a majority of the whole number of electors appointed; and if there be more than one who have such majority, and have an equal number of votes, then the House of Representatives shall immediately choose by ballot one of them for President; and if no person have a majority, then from the five highest on the list the said House shall in like manner choose the President. But in choosing the President, the votes shall be take by States, the representation from each State having one vote; a quorum, for this purpose, shall consist of a member or members from two-thirds of the States, and a majority of all the States shall be necessary to a choice. In every case, after the choice of the President, the person having the greatest number of votes of the electors shall be the Vice President. But if there should remain two or more who have equal votes, the Senate shall choose from them by ballot the Vice President.*

4. The Congress may determine the time of choosing the electors and the day on which they shall give their votes, which day shall be the same throughout the United States.

5. No person except a natural born citizen, or a citizen of the United States, at the

---

* This clause is superseded by Article XII, Amendments.

time of the adoption of this Constitution, shall be eligible to the office of President; neither shall any person be eligible to that office who shall not have attained to the age of thirty-five years, and been fourteen years a resident within the United States.

6. In case of the removal of the President from office, or of his death, resignation or inability to discharge the powers and duties of the said office, the same shall devolve on the Vice President, and the Congress may by law provide for the case of removal, death, resignation or inability, both of the President and Vice President, declaring what officer shall then act as President, and such officer shall act accordingly until the disability be removed, or a President shall be elected.

7. The President shall, at stated times, receive for his services a compensation which shall neither be increased nor diminished during the period for which he shall have been elected, and he shall not receive within that period any other emolument from the United States, or any of them.

8. Before he enters on the execution of his office, he shall take the following oath of affirmation:

"I do solemnly swear (or affirm) that I will faithfully execute the office of President of the United States, and will, to the best of my ability, preserve, protect, and defend the Constitution of the United States."

Sec. 2—1. The President shall be Commander-in-Chief of the Army and Navy of the United States, and of the militia of the several States, when called into the actual service of the United States; he may require the opinion, in writing, of the principal officer in each of the executive departments, upon any subject relating to the duties of their respective offices; and he shall have power to grant reprieves, and pardons for offenses against the United States, except in cases of impeachment.

2. He shall have power, by and with the advice and consent of the Senate, to make treaties, provided two-thirds of the Senators present concur; and he shall nominate and, by and with the advice and consent of the Senate, shall appoint ambassadors, other public ministers and consuls, judges of the Supreme Court, and all other officers of the United States, whose appointments are not herein otherwise provided for, and which shall be established by law; but the Congress may by law vest the appointment of such inferior officers as they think proper in the President alone, in the courts of law, or in the heads of departments.

3. The President shall have power to fill up all vacancies that may happen during the recess of the Senate, by granting commissions which shall expire at the end of their next session.

Sec. 3—He shall from time to time give to the Congress information of the State of the Union, and recommend to their consideration such measures as he shall judge necessary and expedient; he may, on extraordinary occasions, convene both Houses, or either of them, and in cases of disagreement between them with respect to the time of adjournment, he may adjourn them to such time as he shall think proper; he shall receive ambassadors and other public ministers; he shall take care that the laws be faithfully executed, and shall commission all the officers of the United States.

Sec. 4—The President, Vice President, and all civil officers of the United States, shall be removed from office on impeachment for, and conviction of, treason, bribery, or other high crimes and misdemeanors.

Article III

Section 1—The judicial power of the United States shall be vested in one Supreme Court, and in such inferior courts as the Congress may from time to time ordain and establish. The judges, both of the Supreme and inferior courts, shall hold their offices during good behavior, and shall, at stated times, receive for their services a compensation which shall not be diminished during their continuance in office.

Sec. 2—1. The judicial power shall extend to all cases, in law and equity, arising under this Constitution, the laws of the United States, and treaties made, or which shall be made, under their authority;—to all cases affecting ambassadors, other public ministers and consuls; to all cases of admiralty and maritime jurisdiction;—to controversies to which the United States shall be a party;—to controversies between two or more States;—between a State and citizens of another State;—between citizens of different States;—between citizens of the same State, claiming lands under grants of different States, and between a State, or the citizens thereof, and foreign States, citizens, or subjects.

2. In all cases affecting ambassadors, other public ministers and consuls, and those in which a State shall be a party, the Supreme Court shall have original jurisdiction. In all the other cases before mentioned the Supreme Court shall have appellate jurisdiction, both as to law and fact, with such exceptions and under such regulations as the Congress shall make.

3. The trial of all crimes, except in cases of impeachment, shall be by jury, and such trial shall be held in the State where the said crimes shall have been committed; but when not committed within any State the trial shall be at such place or places as the Congress may by law have directed.

Sec. 3—1. Treason against the United States shall consist only in levying war against them, or in adhering to their enemies, giving them aid and comfort. No person shall be convicted of treason unless on the testimony of two witnesses to the same overt act, or on confession in open court.

2. The Congress shall have power to declare the punishment of treason; but no attainder of treason shall work corruption of blood, or forfeiture except during the life of the person attainted.

Article IV

Section 1—Full faith and credit shall be given in each State to the public acts, records, and judicial proceedings of every other State. And the Congress may by general laws prescribe the manner in which such acts, records and proceedings shall be proved, and the effect thereof.

Sec. 2—1. The citizens of each State shall be entitled to all privileges and immunities of citizens in the several States.

2. A person charged in any State with treason, felony, or other crime, who shall flee from justice and be found in another State, shall, on demand of the Executive authority of the State from which he fled, be delivered up, to be removed to the State having jurisdiction of the crime.

3. No person held to service or labor in one State, under the laws thereof, escaping into another, shall, in consequence of any law or regulation therein, be discharged from such service or labor, but shall be delivered upon claim of the party to whom such service or labor may be due.

SEC. 3—1. New States may be admitted by Congress into this Union; but no new State shall be formed or erected within the jurisdiction of any other State; nor any State be formed by the junction of two or more States, or parts of States, without the consent of the Legislatures of the States concerned, as well as of the Congress.

2. The Congress shall have power to dispose of and make all needful rules and regulations respecting the territory or other property belonging to the United States; and nothing in this Constitution shall be so construed as to prejudice any claims of the United States or of any particular State.

SEC. 4—The United States shall guarantee to every State in this Union a republican form of government, and shall protect each of them against invasion, and, on application of the Legislature, or of the Executive (when the Legislature cannot be convened), against domestic violence.

ARTICLE V

The Congress, whenever two-thirds of both Houses shall deem it necessary, shall propose amendments to this Constitution, or, on the application of the Legislatures of two-thirds of the several States, shall call a convention for proposing amendments, which, in either case, shall be valid to all intents and purposes, as part of this Constitution, when ratified by the Legislatures of three-fourths of the several States, or by conventions in three-fourths thereof, as the one or the other mode of ratification may be proposed by the Congress; provided that no amendment which may be made prior to the year one thousand eight hundred and eight shall in any manner affect the first and fourth clauses in the Ninth Section of the First Article; and that no State, without its consent, shall be deprived of its equal suffrage in the Senate.

ARTICLE VI

1. All debts contracted and engagements entered into before the adoption of this Constitution, shall be as valid against the United States under this Constitution, as under the Confederation.

2. This Constitution and the laws of the United States which shall be made in pursuance thereof; and all treaties made, or which shall be made, under the authority of the United States, shall be the supreme law of the land; and the judges in every State shall be bound thereby, anything in the Constitution or laws of any State to the contrary notwithstanding.

3. The Senators and Representatives before mentioned, and the members of the several State Legislatures, and all executive and judicial officers, both of the United States and of the several States, shall be bound by oath or affirmation to support this Constitution; but no religious test shall ever be required as a qualification to any office or public trust under the United States.

ARTICLE VII

The ratification of the Convention of nine States shall be sufficient for the establishment of this Constitution between the States so ratifying the same.

Done in Convention by the Unanimous Consent of the States present the Seventeenth Day of September, in the Year of Our Lord one thousand seven hundred and eighty-seven, and of the Independence of the United States of America the Twelfth. In witness whereof we have hereunto subscribed our names

GEO. WASHINGTON, President and deputy from Virginia, New Hampshire—John Langdon, Nicholas Gilman, Massachusetts—Nathaniel Gorham, Rufus King, Connecticut—Wm. Saml. Johnson, Roger Sherman, New York—Alexander Hamilton, New Jersey—Wil. Livingston, David Brearley, Wm. Patterson, Jona. Dayton, Pennsylvania—B. Franklin, Robt. Morris, Thos. Fitzsimmons, James Wilson, Thomas Mifflin, Geo. Clymer, Jared Ingersoll, Gouv. Morris, Delaware—Geo. Read, John Dickinson, Jaco. Broom, Gunning Bedford, Jr., Richard Bassett, Maryland—James McHenry, Danl. Carroll, Dan. of St. Thos. Jenifer, Virginia—John Blair, Jas. Madison, Jr., North Carolina—Wm. Blount, Hu. Williamson, Richd. Dobbs Spaight, South Carolina—J. Rutledge, Charles Pinckney, Charles Cotesworth Pinckney, Pierce Butler, Georgia—William Few, Abr. Baldwin. Attest: William Jackson, Secretary.

The Constitution was declared in effect on the first Wednesday in March, 1789.

AMENDMENTS TO THE CONSTITUTION OF THE UNITED STATES

The following amendments to the Constitution, Article I to X, inclusive, were proposed at the First Session of the First Congress, begun and held at the City of New York, on Wednesday, March 4, 1789, and were adopted by the necessary number of States. The original proposal of the ten amendments was preceded by this preamble and resolution:

"The conventions of a number of the States having, at the time of their adopting the Constitution, expressed a desire, in order to prevent misconstruction or abuse of its powers, that further declaratory and restrictive clauses should be added, and as extending the ground of public confidence in the Government will best insure the beneficent ends of its institution:

"RESOLVED, By the Senate and House of Representatives of the United States of America, in Congress assembled, two-thirds of both Houses concurring, that the following articles be proposed to the Legislatures of the several States, as amendments to the Constitution of the United States; all or any of which articles, when ratified by three-fourths of the said Legislatures, to be valid to all intents and purposes, as part of the said Constitution, namely":

AMENDMENTS
THE TEN ORIGINAL AMENDMENTS
(Sometimes called our Bill of Rights)
(Declared in force December 15, 1791)

ARTICLE I

Congress shall make no law respecting an establishment of religion, or prohibiting the free exercise thereof; or abridging the freedom of speech or of the press; or the right of the people peaceably to assemble, and to petition the Government for a redress of grievances.

ARTICLE II

A well-regulated militia being necessary to the security of a free State, the right of the people to keep and bear arms shall not be infringed.

ARTICLE III

No soldier shall, in time of peace, be quartered in any house without the consent of the owner, nor in time of war but in a manner to be prescribed by law.

ARTICLE IV

The right of the people to be secure in their persons, houses, papers, and effects, against unreasonable searches and seizures, shall not be violated, and no warrants shall issue, but upon probable cause, supported by oath or affirmation, and particularly describing the place to be searched, and the persons or things to be seized.

ARTICLE V

No person shall be held to answer for a capital or otherwise infamous crime, unless on a presentment or indictment of a grand jury, except in cases arising in the land or naval forces, or in the militia, when in actual service in time of war or public danger; nor shall any person be subject for the same offense to be twice put in jeopardy of life or limb; nor shall be compelled in any criminal case to be a witness against himself, nor be deprived of life, liberty, or property, without due process of law; nor shall private property be taken for public use, without just compensation.

ARTICLE VI

In all criminal prosecutions, the accused shall enjoy the right to a speedy, and public trial, by an impartial jury of the State and district wherein the crime shall have been committed, which district shall have been previously ascertained by law, and be informed of the nature and cause of the accusation; to be confronted with the witnesses against him; to have compulsory process for obtaining witnesses in his favor, and to have the assistance of counsel for his defense.

ARTICLE VII

In suits at common law, where the value in controversy shall exceed twenty dollars, the right of trial by jury shall be preserved and no fact tried by a jury shall be otherwise re-examined in any court of the United States than according to the rules of the common law.

ARTICLE VIII

Excessive bail shall not be required, nor excessive fines imposed, nor cruel and unusual punishments inflicted.

ARTICLE IX

The enumeration in the Constitution of certain rights shall not be construed to deny or disparage others retained by the people.

ARTICLE X

The powers not delegated to the United States by the Constitution, nor prohibited by it to the States, are reserved to the States respectively, or to the people.

ARTICLE XI

The judicial power of the United States shall not be construed to extend to any suit in law or equity, commenced or prosecuted against one of the United States, by citizens of another State, or by citizens or subjects of any foreign State.

(Proposed to the Legislatures of the several states by the Third Congress on the 5th of March, 1794, and declared to have been ratified by Executive Proclamation, January 8, 1798.)

ARTICLE XII

The electors shall meet in their respective States, and vote by ballot for President and Vice President, one of whom at least shall not be an inhabitant of the same States with themselves; they shall name in their ballots the person voted for as President, and in distinct ballots the persons voted for as Vice President; and they shall make distinct lists of all persons voted for as President, and of all persons voted for as Vice President, and of the number of votes for each, which lists they shall sign and certify, and transmit, sealed, to the seat of the Government of the United States, directed to the President of the Senate; the President of the Senate shall, in the presence of the Senate and House of Representatives, open all the certificates, and the votes shall then be counted; the person having the greatest number of votes for President shall be the President, if such number be a majority of the whole number of the electors appointed; and if no person have such majority, then from the persons having the highest numbers, not exceeding three on the list of those voted for as President, the House of Representatives shall choose immediately, by ballot, the President. But in choosing the President, the votes shall be taken by States, the representation from each State having one vote; a quorum for this purpose shall consist of a member or members from two-thirds of the States, and a majority of all the States shall be necessary to a choice. And if the House of Representatives shall not choose a President, whenever the right of choice shall devolve upon them, before the fourth day of March next following, then the Vice President shall act as President, as in the case of the death or other constitutional disability of the President. The person having the greatest number of votes as Vice President shall be the Vice President, if such number be a majority of the whole number of electors appointed, and if no person have a majority, then from the two highest numbers on the list, the Senate shall choose the Vice President; a quorum for the purpose shall consist of two-thirds of the whole number of Senators, and a majority of the whole number shall be necessary to a choice. But no person constitutionally ineligible to the office of President shall be eligible to that of Vice President of the United States.

(Proposed by the Eighth Congress on the 12th of December, 1803, declared ratified by the Secretary of State, September 25, 1804. It was ratified by all the states except Connecticut, Delaware, Massachusetts, and New Hampshire.)

ARTICLE XIII

1. Neither slavery nor involuntary servitude, except as a punishment for crime whereof the party shall have been duly convicted, shall exist within the United States, or any place subject to their jurisdiction.

2. Congress shall have power to enforce this article by appropriate legislation.

(Proposed by the Thirty-eighth Congress on the 1st of February, 1865, declared ratified by the Secretary of State, December 18, 1865. It was rejected by Delaware and Kentucky; was conditionally ratified by Alabama and Mississippi; and Texas took no action.)

ARTICLE XIV

1. All persons born or naturalized in the United States, and subject to the jurisdiction thereof, are citizens of the United States and of the State wherein they reside. No State shall make or enforce any law which shall abridge the privileges or immunities of citizens of the United States; nor shall any State deprive any person of life, liberty, or property, without due process of law; nor deny to any person within its jurisdiction the equal protection of the laws.

2. Representatives shall be apportioned among the several States according to their respective numbers, counting the whole number of persons in each State, excluding Indians not taxed. But when the right to vote at any election for the choice of electors for President and Vice President of the United States, Representatives in Congress, the executive and judicial officers of a State, or the members of the Legislature thereof, is denied to any of the male inhabitants of such State, being twenty-one years of age, and citizens of the United States, or in any way abridged, except for participation in rebellion or other crime, the basis of representation therein shall be reduced in the proportion which the number of such male citizens shall bear to the whole number of male citizens twenty-one years of age in such State.

3. No person shall be a Senator or Representative in Congress, or elector of President and Vice President, or hold any office, civil or military, under the United States, or under any State, who, having previously taken an oath, as a member of Congress, or as an officer of the United States, or as a member of any State Legislature, or as an executive or judicial officer of any State, to support the Constitution of the United States, shall have engaged in insurrection or rebellion against the same, or given aid or comfort to the enemies thereof. But Congress may, by a vote of two-thirds of each House, remove such disability.

4. The validity of the public debt of the United States, authorized by law, including debts incurred for payment of pensions and bounties for services in suppressing insurrection or rebellion, shall not be questioned. But neither the United States nor any State shall assume or pay any debt or obligation incurred in aid of insurrection or rebellion against the United States, or any claim for the loss of emancipation of any slave; but all such debts, obligations, and claims shall be held illegal and void.

5. The Congress shall have power to enforce by appropriate legislation the provisions of this article.

(The Reconstruction Amendment, by the Thirty-ninth Congress on the 16th day of June, 1866, was declared ratified by the Secretary of State, July 28, 1868. The amendment got the support of 23 Northern States; it was rejected by Delaware, Kentucky, Maryland, and 10 Southern States. California took no action. Later it was ratified by the 10 Southern States.)

Article XV

1. The right of the citizens of the United States to vote shall not be denied or abridged by the United States or by any State on account of race, color, or previous condition of servitude.

2. The Congress shall have power to enforce this article by appropriate legislation.

(Proposed by the Fortieth Congress the 27th of February, 1869, and was declared ratified by the Secretary of State, March 30, 1870. It was not acted on by Tennessee; it was rejected by California, Delaware, Kentucky, Maryland and Oregon; ratified by the remaining thirty states. New York rescinded its ratification January 5, 1870. New Jersey rejected it in 1870, but ratified it in 1871.)

Article XVI

The Congress shall have power to lay and collect taxes on incomes, from whatever source derived, without apportionment among the several States, and without regard to any census or enumeration.

(Proposed by the Sixty-first Congress, July 12, 1909, and declared ratified February 25, 1913. The income tax amendment was ratified by all the states except Connecticut, Florida, Pennsylvania, Rhode Island, Utah, and Virginia.)

ARTICLE XVII

1. The Senate of the United States shall be composed of two Senators from each State, elected by the people thereof, for six years; and each Senator shall have one vote. The electors in each State shall have the qualifications requisite for electors of the most numerous branch of the State Legislatures.

2. When vacancies happen in the representation of any State in the Senate, the executive authority of such State shall issue writs of election to fill such vacancies; *Provided*, That the Legislature of any State may empower the Executive thereof to make temporary appointments until the people fill the vacancies by election as the Legislature may direct.

3. This amendment shall not be so construed as to affect the election or term of any Senator chosen before it becomes valid as part of the Constitution.

(Proposed by the Sixty-second Congress on the sixteenth day of May, 1912, and declared ratified May 31, 1913. Adopted by all the states except Alabama, Delaware, Florida, Georgia, Kentucky, Louisiana, Maryland, Mississippi, Rhode Island, South Carolina, Utah and Virginia.)

ARTICLE XVIII

1. After one year from the ratification of this article the manufacture, sale, or transportation of intoxicating liquors within, the importation thereof into, or the exportation thereof from the United States and all territory subject to the jurisdiction thereof for beverage purposes is hereby prohibited.

2. The Congress and the several States shall have concurrent power to enforce this article by appropriate legislation.

3. This article shall be inoperative unless it shall have been ratified as an amendment to the Constitution by the Legislatures of the several States, as provided in the Constitution, within seven years from the date of the submission hereof to the States by the Congress.

(Proposed by the Sixty-fifth Congress, December 18, 1917, and ratified by thirty-six states; was declared in effect on January 16, 1920.)

ARTICLE XIX

1. The right of citizens of the United States to vote shall not be denied or abridged by the United States or by any State on account of sex.

2. Congress shall have power, by appropriate legislation, to enforce the provisions of this article.

(Proposed by the Sixty-fifth Congress. On August 26, 1920, it was proclaimed in effect, having been ratified [June 19, 1919—August 18, 1920] by three-quarters of the states. The Tennessee House, August 31, rescinded its ratification, 47 to 24.)

ARTICLE XX

1. The terms of the President and Vice President shall end at noon on the 20th day of January, and the terms of Senators and Representatives at noon on the 3rd day of January of the years in which such terms would have ended if this article had not been ratified; and the terms of their successors shall then begin.

2. The Congress shall assemble at least once in every year, and such meeting shall begin at noon on the 3rd day of January, unless they shall by law appoint a different day.

3. If, at the time fixed for the beginning of the term of the President, the President elect shall have died, the Vice President elect shall become President. If a President shall not have been chosen before the time fixed for the beginning of his term, or if the President elect shall have failed to qualify, then the Vice President elect shall act as President until a President shall have qualified; and the Congress may by law provide for the case wherein neither a President elect nor a Vice President elect shall have qualified, declaring who shall then act as President, or the manner in which one who is to act shall be selected, and such person shall act accordingly, until a President or Vice President shall have qualified.

4. The Congress may by law provide for the case of the death of any of the persons from whom the House of Representatives may choose a President whenever the right of choice shall have devolved upon them, and for the case of the death of any of the persons from whom the Senate may choose a Vice President when the right of choice shall have devolved upon them.

5. Sections 1 and 2 shall take effect on the 15th day of October following the ratification of this article.

6. This article shall be inoperative unless it shall have been ratified as an amendment to the Constitution by the legislatures of three-fourths of the several States within seven years from the date of its submission.

(Proposed by the Seventy-second Congress, First Session. On February 6, 1933, it was proclaimed in effect, having been ratified by thirty-nine states.)

ARTICLE XXI

1. The eighteenth article of amendment to the Constitution of the United States is hereby repealed.

2. The transportation or importation into any State, Territory, or possession of the United States for delivery or use therein of intoxicating liquors, in violation of the laws thereof, is hereby prohibited.

3. This article shall be inoperative unless it shall have been ratified as an amendment to the Constitution by convention in the several States, as provided in the Constitution, within seven years from the date of the submission hereof to the States by the Congress.

(Proposed by the Seventy-second Congress, Second Session. Proclaimed in effect on December 5, 1933, having been ratified by thirty-six states. By proclamation of the same date, the President proclaimed that the eighteenth amendment to the Constitution was repealed on December 5, 1933.)

ARTICLE XXII

1. No person shall be elected to the office of the president more than twice, and no person who has held the office of president, or acted as president, for more than two years of a term to which some other person was elected president shall be elected to the office of the president more than once. But this article shall not apply to any person holding the office of president when this article was proposed by the Congress, and shall not prevent any person who may be holding the office of president, or acting as president, during the term within which this article becomes operative from holding the office of president or acting as president during the remainder of such term.

2. This article shall be inoperative unless it shall have been ratified as an amendment to the constitution by the legislatures of three-fourths of the several States within seven years from the date of its submission to the States by the congress.

(Proposed by the Eightieth Congress in 1947 and became effective on Feb. 26, 1951, having been ratified by thirty-six states.)

ARTICLE XXIII

1. The District constituting the seat of Government of the United States shall appoint in such manner as the Congress may direct:

A number of electors of President and Vice President equal to the whole number of Senators and Representatives in Congress to which the District would be entitled if it were a State, but in no event more than the least populous State; they shall be in addition to those appointed by the States, but they shall be considered, for the purposes of the election of President and Vice President, to be electors appointed by a State; and they shall meet in the District and perform such duties as provided by the twelfth article of amendment.

2. The Congress shall have power to enforce this article by appropriate legislation.

(Proposed by the Eighty-sixth Congress in June of 1960 and ratified by the thirty-eighth State, March 29, 1961.)

ARTICLE XXIV

1. The right of citizens of the United States to vote in any primary or other election for President or Vice-President, for electors for President or Vice-President or for Senator or Representative in Congress, shall not be denied or abridged by the United States or any State by reason of failure to pay any poll tax or other tax.

2. The Congress shall have the power to enforce this article by appropriate legislation.

(Proposed by the Eighty-seventh Congress in August, 1962, and ratified by the thirty-eighth State January 23, 1964.)

ARTICLE XXV

1. In case of the removal of the President from office or his death or resignation, the Vice-President shall become President.

2. Whenever there is a vacancy in the office of the Vice-President, the President shall nominate a Vice-President who shall take office upon confirmation by a majority vote of both houses of Congress.

54

3. Whenever the President transmits to the President pro tempore of the Senate and the Speaker of the House of Representatives his written declaration that he is unable to discharge the powers and duties of his office, and until he transmits to them a written declaration to the contrary, such powers and duties shall be discharged by the Vice-President as Acting President.

4. Whenever the Vice-President and a majority of either the principal officers of the executive departments or of such other body as Congress may by law provide, transmit to the President pro tempore of the Senate and the Speaker of the House of Representatives their written declaration that the President is unable to discharge the powers and duties of his office, the Vice-President shall immediately assume the powers and duties of the office as Acting President.

Thereafter, when the President transmits to the President pro tempore of the Senate and the Speaker of the House of Representatives his written declaration that no inability exists, he shall resume the powers and duties of his office unless the Vice-President and a majority of either the principal officers of the executive departments or of such other body as Congress may by law provide, transmit within four days to the President pro tempore of the Senate and the Speaker of the House of Representatives their written declaration that the President is unable to discharge the powers and duties of his office. Thereupon Congress shall decide the issue, assembling within 48 hours for that purpose if not in session. If the Congress, within 21 days after receipt of the latter written declaration, or, if Congress is not in session, within 21 days after Congress is required to assemble, determines by two-thirds vote of both houses that the President is unable to discharge the powers and duties of his office, the Vice-President shall continue to discharge the same as Acting President; otherwise, the President shall resume the powers and duties of his office.

(Proposed by the Eighty-ninth Congress in July, 1965, and ratified by the thirty-eighth state February 10, 1967.)

ARTICLE XXVI

1. The right of citizens of the United States, who are eighteen years of age or older, to vote shall not be denied or abridged by the United States or any State on account of age.

2. The Congress shall have the power to enforce this article by appropriate legislation.

(Proposed to the States by Congress on March 23, 1971. Ratification completed June 30, 1971.)

SUGGESTIONS FOR FURTHER READING

Abernethy, Mrs. Max, "Signers of the Declaration," *The State*, XIX (July 7, 1951), 3, 17.

Ashe, Samuel A., and Others (eds), *Biographical History of North Carolina: From Colonial Times to the Present* (Greensboro: Charles L. Van Noppen, 8 volumes, 1905-1917), contains articles on Hewes, Penn, Hooper, Davie, Williamson, Blount, and Spaight.

Dill, Alonzo Thomas, *Governor Tryon and His Palace* (Chapel Hill: The University of North Carolina Press, 1955).

Johnson, Allen, Dumas Malone, and Others (eds.), *Dictionary of American Biography* (New York: Charles Scribner's Sons, 22 volumes and index, 1928—), contains sketches of Hewes, Penn, Hooper, Martin, Davie, Williamson, Blount, and Spaight.

Lawrence, R. C., "Signers of the Constitution," *The State*, X (September 4, 1942), 3, 20.

Lefler, Hugh Talmage, and Albert Ray Newsome, *North Carolina: The History of a Southern State* (Chapel Hill: The University of North Carolina Press, 1963).

Rankin, Hugh F., *North Carolina in the American Revolution* (Raleigh: State Department of Archives and History, 1959).

Sadler, W. J., "Governors of North Carolina—No. 37—Richard Dobbs Spaight," *The State*, III (September 28, 1935), 6.

NC
975.602
M

MLib

NC
975.602
M

DISCARDED
from
New Hanover County Public Library

NEW HANOVER COUNTY PUBLIC LIBRARY
201 CHESTNUT ST.
WILMINGTON, NC   28401